Fantastic Frogs

Written by Liz Miles

Collins

Monster frog

The biggest frog is as big as a cat!
It breeds in pools and rivers.

It can clear rocks from pools with its big strong feet.

Tree frogs

This frog is no bigger than a finger!
It breeds in rainforest trees.

Tree-frog eggs keep moist in pools of rain.

pool

tree frog

eggs

Frogs in flight

This frog hurls itself into the air,
then sails from tree to tree.

6

It clings on to tree trunks with its pads.

Croaking frogs

This frog has a balloon in its throat!
When it fills with air, the frog can croak.

reed frog

Some frogs have a pair of balloons.
Experts think they help frogs float.

Bright frogs

Some frogs have bright skin.
The brightness frightens off attackers.

This plain-looking frog can light up in the dark.

polka dot frog

Is it a frog?

Not all frogs have smooth skin.
This frog looks like moss!

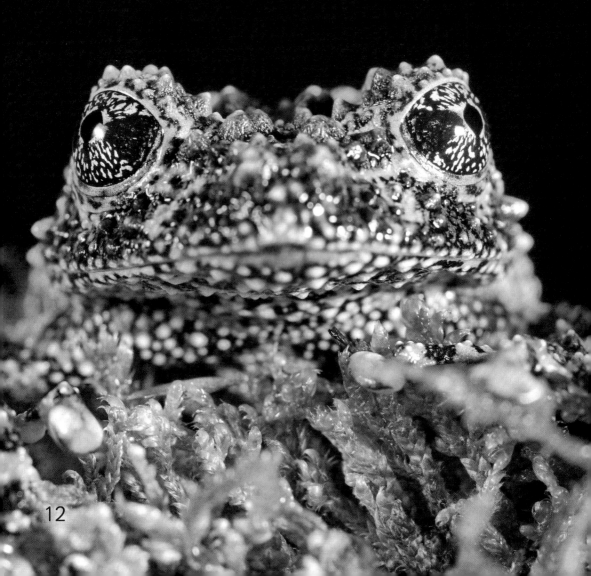

This frog's brown and green skin keeps it hidden at the bottom of the forest.

Fantastic frogs

After reading

Letters and Sounds: Phase 4
Word count: 169
Focus on adjacent consonants with long vowel phonemes, e.g. *trees*.
Common exception words: the, no, of, to, when, some, have, they, all, like
Curriculum links: Science: Animals including humans
National Curriculum learning objectives: Reading/word reading: apply phonic knowledge and skills as the route to decode words; read accurately by blending sounds in unfamiliar words containing GPCs that have been taught; Reading/ comprehension: understand both the books they can already read accurately and fluently and those they listen to by making inferences on the basis of what is being said and done

Developing fluency

- Read pages 2 and 3 aloud to your child, demonstrating an enthusiastic tone and adding emphasis to the surprising fact in the first sentence.
- Take turns to read the rest of the book, with your child reading the left-hand pages, and you reading the right. Check your child notices the commas (for pauses), exclamation marks (extra emphasis) and uses an appropriate tone for the question on page 12.

Phonic practice

- Look at pages 4 and 5 and point to the words with adjacent consonants and long vowel sounds, asking your child to sound out and blend each in turn:

  t/r/ee   b/r/ee/d/s   m/oi/s/t

- Ask your child to reread page 6 but practise reading the words with adjacent consonants, and short and long vowels, first:

  frogs   flight   itself   from   tree

Extending vocabulary

- Challenge your child to suggest two words or phrases with opposite meanings (antonyms) for these:
  o moist (*dry*)
  o bright (e.g. *dull, dark*)
  o plain-looking (e.g. *elaborate-looking, showy*)
  o smooth (e.g. *rough, uneven*)